THE EFFECTS OF DEALING WITH SUICIDE

Dedra Day

authorHOUSE®

AuthorHouse™
1663 Liberty Drive
Bloomington, IN 47403
www.authorhouse.com
Phone: 1-800-839-8640

First published by AuthorHouse   01/21/2011

ISBN: 978-1-4567-1847-3 (sc)
ISBN: 978-1-4567-1848-0 (e)

Library of Congress Control Number: 2011901076

Printed in the United States of America

Any people depicted in stock imagery provided by Thinkstock are models,
and such images are being used for illustrative purposes only.
Certain stock imagery © Thinkstock.

This book is printed on acid-free paper.

This Book is Written In Loving Memory

of

My Beloved Son,

ALEXANDER PAUL GRAHAM!

Alexander Paul Graham
Sept.26,1986- Dec. 7, 2007

MY BELOVED SON

This Book is Dedicated to
My husband, Jeff,
my daughter, Heidi, and my grandchildren!

I LOVE YOU ALL!

A Broken Heart ... a mother's story

Remembering Alex

Alex was not ashamed to admit he was a mommy's boy! I was proud of that! He told a lot of my friends that his mommy was all he had, other than Heidi. Heidi is his sister. We were the only ones who stood by his side, helped him any way we could.

Alex and Heidi were extremely close. He would sometimes talk with her, then he would talk to me. He lived with Heidi and her husband and kids for awhile. She would cook for him, things he liked. And they would go out and do things together. He was also good with Heidi's four kids, Drake, Bryson, Madison and Grayce— they loved their uncle Alex very much. I think her oldest son looks just like Alex.

I remember when Heidi and Alex were little, and we would go places and do things— I remember everything we did back then. Both of them played sports. They loved it! Heidi, when she played Mighty Mites basketball, would walk down the court talking instead of playing ball, and Alex would laugh.

I remember when Alex played T-ball, and Heidi and I would go to his games— I would yell and scream for Alex. One day, a man got up and moved away from me. He said I was too loud. I told him that was my son, and that I was proud of him. Heidi laughed about it for a long time.

I remember when Alex spent the night with one of his friends— they watched the movie "Lost Boys." Alex slept on the top bunk that night, and he woke up screaming. He thought he was floating because he was on the top bunk. We all thought that was cute, but he didn't. He was embarrassed. I told him it was ok, "You're just a little boy." And he loved the Halloween movies! We used to sit and watch every one of them.

I remember when he and Heidi got older, and we went to Wilkes, to the dam, to swim. The girls would watch Alex and flirt with him. I remember all those times.

I remember when they were young, and I worked, and I couldn't afford to get the things they wanted. I would sell my Home Interior off my walls to buy stuff for them. Yes, I spoiled them when they were little, and I am proud to have spoiled them both.

I remember when Alex got his driving license, how I would worry and make him call me when he got to where he was going. That would aggravate him. Then I would keep calling and checking on him. I told him it was a mother's love and nature to worry. (I did the same to Heidi, but when she got to where she was going, she would cut the phone off.) A mother worries about her kids. I did, when mine were out and about.

Alex was proud of his car, and he loved to show it off. He was always working on it or washing and waxing it, or something.

He was very close to his uncle, (my brother) Jeff. He always thought he had to be around Jeff, which was ok, but sometimes Mom wanted quality time also. You know how 21-year-old boys are—they want to do what they want to do and be with whom they want to be with. Alex thought he was big enough to do what he wanted. And he was.

He also spent a lot of time with Jeff's two sons, who were more like brothers than cousins. They were always playing their music loud and doing burnouts. Going to Wilkes' drag strip and running their cars. I used to aggravate him and tell him I could do a better burnout than he could, and he would say, "Bring it on!" I told him I would, at Wilkes' drag strip, where it was legal. He would just laugh and say

I was chicken, and if the truth was told, I was chicken. I didn't want a ticket. He thought it was funny.

I remember when Alex would drive me somewhere, I would be scared to death, not of his driving, but because his little car bounced all over the road because it was so low to the ground. I would tell him, "I am not afraid of your driving—what if someone comes around the curve and you are bouncing and they hit us?" He would laugh and say, "Mom, I know how to drive and handle my car." He always got tickled about that.

Alex liked to joke around and have a good time. He loved to tease his Grandmother Cummings. He would rather pick on her than to eat when he was hungry! But she would always come back with a doozey! They loved to joke around with each other!

He was very thoughtful and kind. He would help anyone he could—he would give you the shirt off his back. He used to work with handicapped people. Sometimes, some of them would need things, and when Alex got paid, he would go and buy it for them. He would help anyone out that he could. I talked with a woman, whose yard Alex used to mow. She said she would take him a washcloth out to wipe his face and take him a drink. She said he was "a precious young man."

Alex was a typical 21-year-old. He had lots of friends and was loved so much and by so many people. He had a good personality and loved life. He was particular about his clothes and hair and teeth. He would shower twice a day and brush his teeth a lot. He had to wear certain clothes, certain cologne. He said he had to look good for the girls.

Alex had the prettiest dimples you have ever seen. Girls loved his smile! He had lots of girl friends and lots of friends. Used to, everywhere you saw Alex, you saw one of his friends with him.

I am not saying Alex was perfect in every way— no one is perfect, but the good Lord. It took a whole lot to make him mad, but when he got mad, he was mad, and you knew it. He didn't care to let you know!

Alex was very protective of his mommy, and he would stand up to anyone over me. I was so proud of that!

When I worked in Boone and would come home, Alex would have the house cleaned and sometimes my supper cooked and the laundry done. Sometimes his two cousins, Mitchell and Derrick, would come and stay. He would say, "If you make a mess, Mom will be mad."

At that time, Heidi was married and lived somewhere else, so it was just me and Alex. He was a good cook— my favorite was his cheesy scrambled eggs— they were delicious! He loved to make brownies and cookies!

And he loved my fried chicken. He would always say, "Mom, will you fry me some chicken? No one makes chicken like you!" I would make him some fried chicken, and he would eat three or four pieces at a time.

Alex was special and very much loved by a lot of people. I carried him in my stomach for nine months and raised him to the best of my knowledge. He was very well-mannered and polite. He and I and Heidi were extremely close. And I never once thought this of Alex, but he was depressed. And he wouldn't ask for help. I wish he would have come to me. I would have gotten him help.

CHAPTER I

On December 6th, 2007, my precious son, Alexander Paul Graham, shot himself. He passed away December 7th, 2007, at 1:15 pm.

On the night of Dec. 6th, my life shattered. I was on the phone with my daughter, Heidi, and she was screaming and yelling for Alex to give her the gun. The next thing I heard was a gunshot. She screamed, "Mommy, he is dead!" I asked her where he had shot himself. She said, "In the head." I told her to call 911 and then call me back. I had no car.

I called my boyfriend, Jeff (now my husband) who was in Salisbury, NC, on a job, and then I called my parents. Jeff's mom, Naomi, and his sister, Sandy, came to be with me, and my best friend, Ruby, came over to me— I took her to the ground. She waited with me until my mom and dad came, then we went to the hospital. I waited what seemed to be forever before the ambulance got there. They wouldn't even let me see my baby. They put him straight on a helicopter and flew him to Johnson City Medical Center, in Johnson City, TN. I called my sister, Kathy, who lives in Castlewood, VA, and asked her if she could go there and await for the helicopter that had Alex, and she did.

Jeff got me and took me straight to Johnson City Medical, where they took me and Alex's dad up to see him. I couldn't believe it. That didn't look like my son lying there with tubes and IVs and cotton up his nose and a breathing machine. My preacher and his wife went with us to Johnson City and stayed with me until about 6 a.m. They were there for me and are wonderful people. For that, I thank God.

They told us we would have to wait and talk with the neurologist at 6 a.m. The doctor said Alex was brain dead, but they would run some tests to see if there was any blood flow to the brain.

Heidi and I would go into Alex's room and talk with him, and his blood pressure would go up. One time, he moved, and I asked the nurse, "Did you see that?" She said, "Yes." I asked if that was good or bad and she said she didn't know. They came back and told us there was no blood flow, that he was gone.

I went crazy, screaming and crying—I even threw up on myself. They ran me out of ICU, said I was scaring the other patients. But losing a child to suicide is so devastating and more intense and complicated and prolonged—my heart was shattered into millions of tiny pieces. Trying to cope with it all at once is very hard. Thank God for Jeff. I would have never made it without him. He stood by my side and cleaned me up when I threw up all over myself. He never left my side for a week or longer.

They told me I could go back in (to see Alex) as long as I was quiet. Heidi and I stayed with him for hours after he had passed. The hospital kept him breathing because we donated his organs. At the time, I was so upset I didn't know—my mind was scrambled. I looked at Heidi, and I looked at Jeff, and they both talked to me about it, and Heidi and I decide to donate his organs. He saved 6 people's lives. See, his dad was not there. He left after 1-1/2 hours of being there. Alex's dad is sick with seizures.

They told me I could stay with Alex (at the hospital) while they where getting his organs, so I could still see him when I could. But my family and my husband said no. Jeff had to take me out in a wheelchair. I wanted to be with Alex! I didn't want to leave him.

We had to call and tell Alex's dad that he was gone. He got there after we had all left. That is when things got harder for me and Heidi. His dad wanted everything his way or no way at all. I only got to pick out the casket and the cards. His dad decided everything else. He made us wait to bury Alex and he was really swollen. When Alex got to the funeral home, I went two or three times a day to see him. He died on the 7th and was not buried until the 15th. You know, a parent is always prepared to go before their kids, but that is not the case all the time.

Alex was a good young man. At age 21, he had lots of friends and was well loved by a lot of people. But he was also mistreated by some—talked about, accused of stealing their property (when, in reality, someone else did). You know, they say that losing someone will always get easier, but take it from someone who knows— IT DOESN'T!

I think of Alex every day. I talk to his pictures, and I even wear his cologne sometimes. I miss his phone calls and him asking me for things, or me making his lunch for work. I can remember every little detail, and it has been 28 months since I lost him. I remember all the good times we had and all the things we did and places we went. I have his car and his clothes—I even have the clothes they cut off him that night. I look at the pictures when he was in the hospital and of the funeral. I listen to songs we both liked, and I just cry. I get his clothes out and smell them and hold them—some I wear. Others smell like him and I just smell them.

I fixed Alex's grave really beautiful! It has red cinderblocks around it to the headstone and is filled in with white gravel. It has two solar crosses that light up at night. Everybody took a fit over the way I did it. They say it's really pretty. I hope Alex is proud of me.

I go to New River Behavioral center, where I have a wonderful therapist, but I don't care much for my psychiatrist. He tells me to move on and forget my son. That will never happen. I asked him, "Have you ever lost a child?" He said, "No." I told him, "Then you do not know what I am going through."

I will not take antidepressants! God's love and the love of my husband, my daughter, grandkids and my preacher and his wife help me through it. I have never one time questioned God. Never. I just ask God to help me understand. God and my husband have helped me through this.

You know, there are times I wonder if I was with Alex, if I could have stopped him! There are times I worry about my daughter and what she saw that night and things she has had to go through. She will not talk about him much. She says he is in Heaven, not in the grave. True, but it is respectful to go visit a loved one's grave, I believe.

CHAPTER 2

Suicide survivors— who are they? They are mothers, fathers, sisters, brothers, nieces and nephews, etc.

We all think it could never happen to us! Yet, we see it everywhere. When it does happen to you, you think your heart is crushed into millions of tiny pieces.

People say it's pain that only time can heal! But for me, time has not healed any!

Those who have lost a child have days they feel as though they're not going to make it. Will it ever get better? And there are times, what if? What if I was there? Could I have stopped him? What could I have done differently to have helped him? What if I had done things differently with him? Maybe I should have been more strong, and strict, and monitored who he dated and hung out with. But he was a well-loved young man! So I never thought Alex would do anything like that! Alex loved Life! Even though people talked bad about him, and stole off of Alex! And they were people close to him, and that hurt him!

I am the type of mom that would stand up to the biggest man and fight for my kids. I never let anyone walk all over my kids. Never.

If they were wrong, I would say so, but if they were right, there was a fight.

The grieving process for everyone is different. People need to deal with it in their own ways. My way of grieving is talking to Alex's pictures, visiting his grave, looking at pictures and talking about him and remembering all the good times. Sometimes, I feel that people do not want to hear anything about him, and that really hurts me. So I have gone back to holding it in and just crying when I am alone, and I don't talk about him to anyone but my therapist!!

I feel so discouraged when I go places where he hung out and see some of his friends and others there, and My Baby is gone! I miss him so much, but I wouldn't bring him back to this cold cruel world. Alex told Heidi and me he would marry his first love! But that never happened. I will never see Alex marry! I will never have any grandkids by Alex!

Chapter 3

I have had several people, who are real religious, tell me that God told them Alex is with him!!!!! One was my Aunt Freda. She was my inspiration. She knew the Bible like no one else I know. She was always there for me to talk to, but she passed away from cancer one year and about 20 days after Alex. Then another woman, who talked in tongues, told me the same thing. She was one of Alex's friend's grandmother. She really loved Alex—he helped her out a lot.

I keep a lot of mementos nearby. I have a lot of pictures, his birth certificate and his death certificate, and a lot of his stuff sitting around. I carry his pictures, even the ones from when he was gone (taken at the hospital) and ones of his funeral. I look at them a lot. I have the DVD from the funeral home and one that my friend Ruby made me that I watch a lot!!!! There are a few songs I listen to that were played at his viewing and funeral, and other songs that we liked together. I do this when I am alone. I don't want to make anyone feel they have to watch or listen to them.

I miss him so much!!! I pray, and when I talk to his pictures, I ask him to come to me, so I can see him. If it's God's will, Alex will come to me. My daughter sees Alex a lot, and he talks with her. He told her he loved her, and to tell me he loved me and for her to take care of me.

Then there was a stranger who came into my home (he is now married to a family member), who told me my son was annoying! I got ticked. He said, "No, I'm sorry. He was very persistent! He said he wanted me to come tell you he loves you and he wants to come see you."

Well, when you lose a child, you hope for a lot of things. This made me excited. I said, "Yes!!!!!!!!!!!!!!" Then he came back in two days and told me that Alex wasn't ready, and asked, was me and Alex fighting before he passed? I said, no, we where very close. He said that is what my niece had said and he felt Alex didn't want to see me. I was crushed. I called several people and asked them if Alex loved me? They said 'yes,' and that Alex always said I was all he had to rely on. So I called my preacher and talked with him. He said that Satan could be working through that guy, or they could be doing it to hurt me, and to tell them I didn't want to hear any more—and I did.

Sometimes I sit and worry and cry over my daughter, Heidi. Alex was at her house when he shot himself in the head. What all my girl saw and went through that night! They tested her hands for gun residue even after what she saw. Then she had to help carry out the mattress and burn it because of all the blood. Her home had the bullet holes in the walls from one room to another. She witnessed a lot! But she will not discuss it. She blames herself for not getting the gun away from Alex. I told her I was glad she didn't fight him, or I could have lost them both. But she doesn't see it that way. She thinks she should have gotten the gun!

I told her I was on the phone with her, I heard her, she tried. But the next thing we heard, in between her screaming for Alex to give her the gun, was a gunshot! I have tried to get her to go to New

River Mental Health with me, but she will not. She says she doesn't want to talk about it! But when she sees Alex and talks with him, I tell her, he is letting her know he is ok, and he loves her, and it's not her fault. But she is carrying a lot on her.

For several weeks, Heidi wouldn't go to her house alone. She didn't stay there for weeks. She only went to get clothes and stuff for her and the kids. When she did start back staying at home, she called me one evening and said, "Mom, you're going to think I am crazy!" I said, "What?" She said, "I seen Alex!" He was standing in her bedroom, and she was in her bathroom (which had double doors that were open). She said Alex told her he loved her, and to tell (me) he loved (me). She started crying and screaming, "Alex, I love you!" and shut her eyes. When she opened her eyes, he was gone. She even said he had on his black 'wife beater' shirt, as they call them, and his jeans. That was the shirt he had on the night he committed suicide. I have the shirt and stuff he was in, and the blanket. She has seen him a couple more times even though she moved, and moved out of Ashe County.

Heidi has four children, two boys and two girls. The oldest is a boy, then the two girls, and her baby is a boy. Well, her third child says she talks to Uncle Alex all the time. She woke Heidi up at 5 a.m. one morning and said, "Mommy, I thought Uncle Alex was in Heaven?" Heidi said, "Yes, he is." Her little girl said, "He's in my room, watching cartoons with me." She told her, "Uncle Alex comes and checks on you all and then goes back to Heaven. But Uncle Alex always watches over us all!!!!!!"

CHAPTER 4

Survivors of suicide need healing after a loved one's death. As the mother of a son who committed suicide, it is very devastating and emotional. It's harder to deal with a suicide death. There are so many unanswered questions.

Grieving after a loved one's death from suicide is more complicated, intense and prolonged then a death by natural causes—someone with a sickness such as cancer or some other disease. You have feelings of shock, confusion, anger, despair, grief, guilt and a lot of 'what ifs.' Shock is disbelief, that it is all a bad dream and when you wake up, it will all be gone! But when you do wake up, it's still there. And the disbelief for me is still with me.

My husband says I talk to Alex in my sleep, and he answers me (as if he were Alex). I have good dreams and I have bad dreams. Trying to deal with what the dreams mean, or what made you have those dreams. Shock is also trying to deal with what we think is a nightmare and why people don't understand, like I do. Why they don't hurt like I do!

Confusion is trying to understand why someone would commit suicide, especially when they loved life and had lots of friends and had a wonderful personality. A person who loved joking around, and a person who would lend any of his friends a helping hand. Confusion is also why people don't want to talk about the person or go visit their grave. I know everyone grieves differently, but I think it helps to talk about good memories, and to go visit the grave and keep it up and looking nice.

There is also anger—I have no anger towards Alex, but at others. I also have anger and hurt because I felt I didn't have all the family support that I needed. Alex loved all his family, but some family members didn't even shed a tear over him! That angered me a lot. And I let them know, after he was buried, how I felt. I feel anger when I see friends and others at places where he hung out. And I am angry he is not there! I have anger because people have some of his belongings and won't give them to me. Alex just left (the belongings) at their house. I have anger at people who say they hurt more over Alex than I do—that is ludicrous!!!!!!!!!!!!!!

Despair, sadness, depression and feeling hopeless— even thoughts of suicide. I have a lot of sadness, and I am depressed. I go to New River Mental Health and talk with professionals. I have Major Depressive Disorder, Recurrent Generalized Anxiety Disorder and Post Traumatic Stress Disorder. And it's hard, very hard! I still cry every day over Alex. I talk to his pictures. I can remember the exact times of everything that happened. Also, watching movies or TV programs where a young man committed suicide like Alex, is very difficult to handle and deal with. It brings it all back, fresh, in my head, just like that day.

I pray, and ask Alex all the time to come see me. My preacher said, if it's God's will, Alex will come. There are days I don't even care if I get dressed or go out of the house. But with the love of my wonderful husband and daughter and grandkids, and most of all, God—they all give me strength on the other days. I have never thought of suicide, but I say, "I wish I was with Alex." I have a loving husband and a wonderful daughter and four great grandkids. But if it hadn't been for my husband and daughter and four grandkids, I might have done it. They are my life support.

Guilt. I feel guilty sometimes, wondering if I had been there, could I have stopped him? If I was there, could we have talked and solved what was bothering him? What if he had stayed with me? He had been with me that day for several hours, and I took pictures of him, and we spent quality time together. I wonder why I didn't see something bothering him and if I could have, could I have done something to help him? My husband tells me to quit blaming myself.

I feel guilty because I don't have his car fixed the way he wanted it. But I can't get anyone to work on it. It means a lot to me to get it fixed because Alex's car was his pride and joy. But it has not been fixed after 28 months. He was proud of his 1996 Eagle Talon. He had a racing chip in it, and it would run fast!!! I wanted to fix it back the way he had it. See, his timing belt broke— everyone says I need a motor. I don't know. But I want it fixed so I can drive it with PRIDE!!

I feel guilt because it seems like all his friends have forgotten him. I don't understand how anyone could forget him. I know they have to go on with their lives, but don't forget Alex! He was a very special young man. Oh, how I miss Alex!

CHAPTER 5

Dealing with the anniversary of a loved one's death is tremendously hard. Every month, the day he shot himself and the day he died are extremely difficult. And then when it comes to the same month and the same day, that makes it even more difficult.

All holidays are hard. You never want to get into the spirit of the holiday. It's even more difficult if your loved one commits suicide right before a major holiday like Christmas. It's hard, any way you go. You go through bouts of crying, screaming, angry outbursts and total physical exhaustion. There are times you don't care whether you get out of bed or not.

Emotions come weeks, months and even years after losing a child or family member to suicide. You can develop Post Traumatic Stress Disorder (which I have). This includes nightmares, flashbacks, and social withdrawal (avoiding people and family who remind you of your loved one). Problems sleeping, can't concentrate, no motivation, loss of interest in daily activities or hobbies, family arguments or conflicts, even denial of emotional feelings and pain.

Pain that never goes away, even though people say it does, with time. 28 months and my pain is the same. I really have to make myself get ready for the holidays, but I do, for my husband, my daughter and my grandkids.

Sometimes I feel like my family doesn't care (but I know better)! Everyone grieves differently, and some I can't even get to go to the grave with me. I feel I need more family support. Suicide is awful! The event is burnt into your mind and you really can't get rid of it. No one understands unless they have been through it. That is why I am writing this. It helps me, and maybe, if anyone reads this, it will help them, also.

Chapter 6

In the United States each year, over 33,000 people commit suicide. According to statistics, in Ashe County, North Carolina, from January 2001 to date a minimum of 287 people completed, attempted or threatened suicide. In 2009, Ashe County was rated Number 1 for the number of suicides (per capita) in North Carolina. In 2009, there were 8 completed suicides and 15 attempts or threatened. In 2010, based on unofficial statistics, there have been a minimum of 5 completed. And that is not including accidental overdoses or other self-inflicted deaths that were unreported. My son was one in 2007.

Ashe County has a program to try and prevent suicides from happening, Ashe Suicide/Depression Awareness and Prevention (ASAP) Task Force, and also a program to help survivors of suicide. ASAP is there to let people know it is OK to ask for HELP!!!! There is a crisis line you can call for help. It is 336-246-HEAL (4325). I am joining the ASAP committee, and I am hoping I will be able to help someone. I also hope Alex is looking down at me and saying, "Yeah, that's my Mom!" and that I am making him proud.

We are doing all we can to help! I think every county in the United States should have something like ASAP. I just started to help do a few things— I try my best. But the pain never goes away. We try to let everyone know asking for help is OK.

ASAP has awareness walks, and they have candlelight vigils for the families and friends, where you can bring pictures and mementos to share. You can also speak about your loved one. I have walked the Walk and I talked at the Candlelight Vigil—I spoke about Alex. I hope I can help keep someone else from committing suicide. And I hope Alex is looking down on me, and I am making him proud of me.

They also have a newsletter they send out, with information, and it has a section called 'In Loving Memory' where you can have them put in a picture of your loved one if you want. The survivors group meets every month on the second Monday. Other survivors are there to talk with you and share with you and try to help you.

Suicide is so traumatic! You can't always see the person is depressed and you never know anything is bothering them. So when they do commit suicide, it is such a traumatic shock, especially when you just talked with them about 15 minutes before and they told you they loved you and would see you in the morning. You would never expect minutes later for that person to have committed suicide.

A lot of teens and young people commit suicide over losing a love, or should I say a person they are in love with or dating, and get their heart broken? Some, because they feel hopeless and like they will never amount to anything. There are so many different reasons they feel the need for suicide, when in reality, all they need to do is ask for help. But they are too embarrassed or feel too proud to ask for HELP. No one should be embarrassed or feel too proud! Everyone needs someone to talk to at points in their life. It may be hard, but in the long run, it's worth it to ASK FOR HELP!!

CHAPTER 7

Some survivors struggle or are embarrassed to tell people their loved one committed suicide. You may find it helps to reach out to friends and family because some people don't know how to react to death, especially suicide. For me, I live with the loss, the tragedy and the gaping hole in my heart! There is no closure, nor would I want there to be. I want to remember Alex all my life! I want to remember his smile, his beautiful dimples, his great sense of humor, his pride of always looking good and smelling good. His phone conversations with me. His clothes, the way they smell, his laughter and all the good times we had. Even though it is still very hard on me.

Alex is a hero to me!!! He saved 6 peoples lives:

Alex's heart went to a 43-year-old man, who is married and has 5 children. This man got a wonderful heart! It was successful, thank God.

Alex's right kidney went to a 73-year- old man, who is married with one child. It was successful, thank God.

Alex's left kidney went to a 46-year-old man, now gone back to work. He has been married for 24 years. It was successful, thank God.

Alex's liver went to a 60-year-old woman, who is a widow. She has a son and a 6-year-old grandson. It was successful, thank God.

Alex's pancreas went to a 50-year-old man, who is married with 3 children. He is a police officer. It was successful, thank God.

Alex's left lung went to a 50-year-old man. It was successful, thank God.

Alex's right lung collapsed, so it couldn't be used!

I got a letter from the man who received one of Alex's kidneys. He said Alex gave him the gift of life. The transplant was done on his birthday, and that was the best birthday he ever had other then the day he was born. I felt so proud of Alex! Yet, my heart still ached.

Chapter 8

You know, I talked about the anniversary of a loved one's death. I went up around the first of the month to see how much damage the snow had done to Alex's grave where I have it fixed. I couldn't get anyone to go with me. It had been awhile since I had been there, due to weather. I saw it needed some work, so I went back a few days later and I fixed it. Once again, I went alone—no one would go with me. Well, I truly lost it! It was just like the night it happened. And when I hit the road home, I went real fast, I didn't care if I wrecked or what! Then I thought of my wonderful husband at work and my daughter and grandkids, and I slowed down.

I don't understand why none of my family want to go to the grave with me, and that hurts and angers me a lot. Alex was my baby and they're kin; they should want to go out of respect for Alex, if not for me! Well, like I said, each month on the 6th and 7th, it's extremely hard for me. On the 7th, I went to Alex's grave and took flowers and two balloons (one said, "I love you," and the other was just a red heart). My sister, Liz, went with me that day. We took pictures, and I cried. I told her the hardest thing I have ever had to do is leave Alex! I know he is in a better place, but my heart is still broken into millions of tiny pieces. I went Saturday, May 1st, to Alex's grave and took a blanket and just lay beside his grave and talked with him. I miss him so much!

I was cleaning yesterday and cleaning his flowers I have from the funeral and his pictures. I talked to him and told him I loved him. I listened to music that we both love and just talked away to him.

I am writing this because it helps me. I remember everything right down to the minute we left Johnson City Medical Center. And by me writing this, and someone reading it and it helping them, I will be proud. Because that is what I want it to do—HELP others. I hope to help another parent from going through what I did. I don't wish that on anyone, not even people I don't care for, but I pray for God to touch their souls and for them to see their sins and to ask for forgiveness from God. I don't wish it on them—NEVER!

It is too hard and traumatic, and no one really deserves to go through this. If only people would ask for help and not be embarrassed or too proud. I know God has all our days limited on this earth, and God knows everything. He never puts more on you then you can bear. Well, Alex committing suicide brought me closer to God! I am proud to be a child of God. I am trying to get my daughter to get her life right with God and to come to church and bring the grandchildren. God will give me the wisdom and the knowledge that I need to succeed.

You know, God is an awesome God, and He can do anything. He will answer our prayers in His time. So you see why I tell you God and His love has helped me through this. I can talk with God by prayer and going to church and praying, and that lets me know He loves me, His child, and He will always be with me!

CHAPTER 9

Alex's funeral was really hard. I had to put a hat on him so the bullet holes couldn't be seen. And he was so swollen, where his dad made us wait. One thing really got to me—it was this poem that was read at Alex's funeral by my niece:

"If Alex could, I know he would say, 'Don't weep for me because I'm okay;

To my friends and family, please be thankful today;

I'm still close beside you in a very special way.

I love you all so dearly, now please don't shed a tear, because I want to tell you

I'm spending Christmas with Jesus this year.

I still hear the songs, I still see the lights, I still feel your love on cold winter's nights.

I'll still share your hopes and all your cares, I'll even remind you to say your prayers;

Because I came here before you to help set your place.

So don't weep for me, no, not one tear, just stay in God's grace.

I know how much you'll miss me, I see the pain inside your heart;

But I'm not far away, we're really not apart.

So be happy for me, my dear loved ones, you know I hold you dear,

And please be glad for me because I'm spending Christmas with Jesus this year.

But I sent you all a gift, from my new Heavenly home above;

I sent you each a memory of my undying love.

Please love and keep each other as my Savior said to do,

For I can't count the blessings or love He has for each of you.

So, Merry Christmas, and wipe away those tears,

For I want you all to remember, I'm spending Christmas with Jesus this year.

Love, Alex.

P.S. I love you, Mom, Jeff, Heidi, Dad, Russell, Drake, Madison, Gracye, Bryson, Grandma, Grandpa and all the family and friends."

This really got to me! Alex would have said don't shed a tear for him, to be happy. But I was aching inside, and I knew my boy! I had a lot of unanswered questions, but God's love and my prayers helped me with this. You see, Christmas is extremely hard on me and my daughter, but she is such a wonderful mother, she pushes on and holds it all in. She says she has to be strong for her kids! And I totally agree. Parents are never ready to lose a child, so parents, what I am saying is, cherish your children and love them unconditionally! You never know when they might not be here.

I wish I could have talked with Alex about what was bothering him, but I did talk to him 15 minutes on the phone before he did it, and I never expected anything like this. He told me he loved me and would see me in the morning. My point is, don't ever take life for granted—or your family! Cherish your children! Never think it won't happen to you because you never know. Kids are a precious gift from God. All family is a precious gift! Love each other like it was your last day because you never know—it could be!

It's hard to lose a child! We had no burial insurance or anything like that, so I had several benefit yard sales and bake sales combined, and I also had a benefit pinto bean supper. Ashe County newspapers were wonderful! They put articles in the papers for me, and they also took donations that came in. I wrote a thank-you piece to put in the paper to thank all the people who helped and donated. Here is what it said:

"To The Jefferson Post, I want to thank you for putting in such a wonderful article about my son's benefit supper, bake sale and singing. Thank you very much! I also want to thank Welcome Home Baptist Church for their love and support. I want to thank the community, to those who came and ate and paid and gave donations, and those who just came and dropped off donations. I want to thank all of you for helping and supporting my family in a devastating time for me, the loss of my son (my baby), a good young man. There are not enough words to express my thanks and gratitude. All I can say is, I thank you from the bottom of my heart, and I greatly appreciate everything so much! It's nice to know in a tragedy like this, you have a community that cares. Once again, thank you to everyone, and may God bless you all! Dedra, Alex Graham's Mother."

Chapter 10

There are days that I sit and think about the day my kids were born. Heidi was born August 7, 1983, and Alex was born September 26, 1986. When they were little, everyone thought they were twins. Heidi was so small and fragile, and Alex was average size—so they thought they were twins.

My kids were very special. When their dad and I divorced, I got custody of the kids, so I took care of them and raised them. Their dad got them every other weekend, and most of the time they didn't want to go. But I made them, so they could be with their dad. I didn't want to keep them from him. But when they got old enough, I didn't make them go unless he pitched a fit. He would sometimes get them and then call me and tell me to come get this 'Momma's Boy.' We would fight and argue right in the middle of the road. Alex wanted to stay with me. Heidi never really gave a fit until she started dating, then she didn't want to go.

Heidi and Alex were very close, and they got even closer as they grew up. Yes, they were like other brothers and sisters that argue occasionally, but they always were there for each other.

Alex was real good with Heidi's kids! He loved them and played with them, and would even babysit them from time to time. Her youngest one called Alex "Papaw" until after he passed. One day, out of the blue, he looked at Alex's picture and said, "Uncle Alex is in heaven." I said, "Yes." Heidi and I were both taken by that. His death really affected them all.

A couple of days before Alex's birthday, Heidi and I took them to his grave. They wrote notes and I brought helium balloons and they let them go. Then we all worked on his grave. That meant a lot to me and to them.

Heidi and Alex and I were very close—I love my kids so much. Alex's death affected a lot of people. He is gone, but he will NEVER EVER be forgotten. We all love you and miss you, Alex.

I hope this book will help someone who is depressed and thinking suicide to rethink, and just ask for help. Life is too precious! Thank you!

Mother by love, not blood

Alex has always been like a second son to me. Since he and my son, Steven, were seven or eight years old, they were inseparable. They were so much alike—if one was up to something, you could bet the other was there, too. When they were thirteen, Alex and my daughter, Ashley tried to "date." But it didn't work because they were too much like brother and sister. They always loved each other and watched out for each other.

As they all grew up, they developed different relationships. But they always knew if they ever needed each other, they would be there. The night Alex committed suicide, it was a shock. Alex was always such a fun-loving kid. He always had a joke or a funny story to tell. He was always so full of energy and love. He could make you laugh no matter how bad your day or how mad he could make you sometimes. When he died, it was like a part of my heart died. It felt as if I had lost one of my own kids.

Alex, I love you, and truly believe I'll see you again one day.

"Mom" Ruby

Broken heart by your best friend!!!!!!!!
Cousin and Best friends story:

I remember when Alex was young, My mom would go and get Alex and bring him home to stay all night. We were always real close. We would ride go karts up and down the road and go to the neighbors and aggravate them. We would always hang around cars even when we was little. We always wanted to be with my Dad in his hot rod cars. We tried to make go karts into hot rods. But it didn't work out so well!

My mom would go and take Alex when his Mom said no, because Mom wanted Alex there. Alex always wanted to be with me and we would play.

When we got older we were more into cars then ever. My first car was a 1978 cutlass and Alex's was a MR2 we would piddle with the cars and tear stuff up. We would sit in the cars and listen to the radio for hours. It was our time to talk and be young boys.

Aunt Dede caught me and Alex smoking one time in the woods. Boy she wore our butts out. Aunt Dede told us she rather us smoke in front of her then behind her back. But she didn't want us to. We was around 13 or 14 years old. But we didn't smoke no more.

Alex was there for me when my Mom passed away, he loved Mom just like she was his mom and he loved me like a brother.

As we got older we got more into cars and racing and getting tickets and we thought we were all that!!!!!! But we got fooled: we got a ticket with no drivers licenses. But did we learn NO!

We went to Alabama Alex got so mad because Aunt Dede wouldn't race other Imports on a six lane highway. But Aunt Dede did go after one though. Alex was proud of his car. We always was working on it and cleaning or trying to put things on it to make it go faster. Alex was my Best Friend even though we were first cousins. When you seen one you seen the other. We use to work the Auto Auction on Thursday nights just so we would have gas money to go to town and find some races. We even went to Wilkes drag strip and raced our cars. When we were around 16.

As we got older and was dating we still was real close. If I needed him he came, if he needed me I went.

My wife Brittany has memories of Alex. Alex stayed with me and her some and they got close. She and Alex made me make chocolate chip pancakes at 11' o'clock at night. I didn't want to but I did it any way. Alex would sometimes Pick Brittany up from college when she didn't have a way home. If Alex wanted to come to the house and I wasn't home. He would call and ask me if it was alright. I would tell him yeah go ahead. We always trusted each other.

I lived with Aunt Dede and them in the beginning of 1999. My Mom passed away in 1998 and I went to live with Aunt Dede.

Alex and I would have people over and sometimes they would be 4 or 5 of us in the bed. That was hard but we managed. We had a lot of friends stay over. Aunt Dede would always say don't drink all my Mtn. Dew and clean up your mess when she would go to work.

We would clean and cook supper. Alex was the cook. Alex was a good cook. I miss Alex so much!

On the night of December 6th 2007 was a horrible night! I thought I was having a bad dream, But I wasn't. My Best friend took his own life. Aunt Dede called me and told me. Brittany and I went to Ashe Memorial Hospital and waited with everyone else for the ambulance. It seemed like it took for ever. Then when it did get there they put him straight on a helicopter and flew straight to Johnson City Medical center. They was about hundred of people at ashe memorial and about 80 at Johnson city. Everyone hoping that he would be alright. When I first seen him at Johnson City, it didn't even look like Alex, it was a nightmare. I walked out I couldn't handle it no more. The thought of My Best friend just lying in there. My heart fell to my feet when they told me he was gone. I felt my heart breaking, just like when my mom passed. I had lost my Best Friend. I was hoping I would wake up from this nightmare But I didn't. It was real, all to real. A couple weeks after Alex passed, Brittany and I got into a argument and I took off in my car and exceed the speed limit by 130 miles a hour and looked in the rear view mirror and there was Alex, He told me to slow down and go home. That everything would be alright. Still to this day I still find myself trying to call his phone and Knowing my Best Friend is gone. When I work on my car it get more difficult because I wonder what would Alex would do different or what he would think of what I was doing. If I can't get something to work, I say if Alex was here we could get it to work.

I could tell something was bothering Alex. But I didn't know it was that bad. He didn't talk about it much. But I had a feeling of what it was! But I didn't think it would lead to that! I didn't know he was suffering from Depression. I just wished he would of talked to me or someone and ask for help. It is still pretty hard on me. I have no one to talk to like I did Alex. I love you and miss you my Best Friend. You are held close in my heart and always will be. You are gone but NOT FORGOTTEN!!!

— Love Mitchell and Brittney

Stop, think, live...

Alex is my nephew. He always made over me. In my heart, no one was worthy of Alex's love. He was so special!

The night they called me and said he had shot himself, it was like someone had hit me in my stomach, more so, in my heart. On the way to the hospital, my heart hurt so badly. I kept thinking, this is not real. I had to be dreaming. But it was all too real. Alex passed away the next day.

Alex would ask me to pray for him, or we would get together in Mom's kitchen and I would pray for him. I wish I could tell Alex that nothing is worth taking your life over. God is always with you and loves you unconditionally.

He had a beautiful smile and those sweet dimples. Alex's Dad took a week to bury him. It was so hard just seeing him lying there. The whole time I just wanted him to get up and go home with me.

Alex's death really hurt his mother. It has been almost three years, and she is still suffering from a broken heart. Losing a child is hard, but to lose him by his own hand is devastating.

If you get depressed, down and out, please talk to someone! It doesn't matter to who—just talk. You know, God is always, always listening. He will help—all you have to do is the asking. When Alex died, it hurt so many people. He was loved by a lot of people.

I want everyone to stop and think, before you do something that will hurt everyone you love. There is so much for you to live for. Remember all those people who love you and the big hole that will be in their heart and their lives. Please just stop and think!

Alex will always hold a special place in my heart and in my life.

I will always love you, Alex. Forever.

—Your Aunt Kathy

Note: The reason you didn't hear from my husband, Jeff, is because it still affects him to this day! Jeff loved Alex and misses him a lot.

Dedra Day

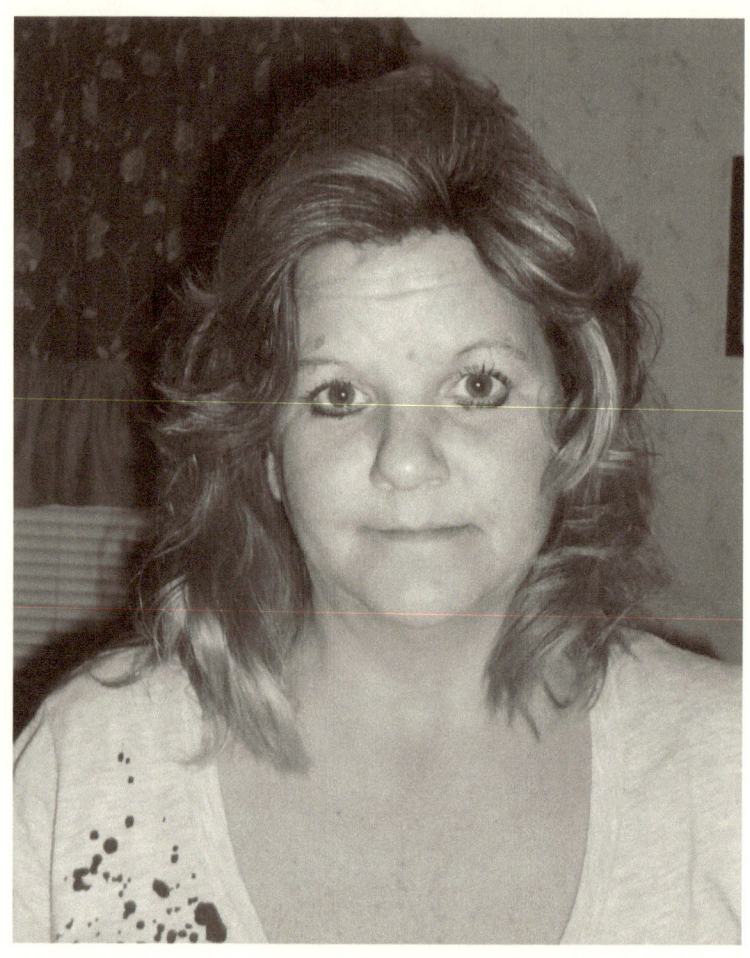

About Dedra Day

I was born in Manassas, Virginia.I have 3 brothers and 2 sisters. At the age of 10 we moved to the Mountains in Whitetop Virginia.I married and had 2 wonderful kids.We Divorced in 1988. I had custody of the kids. I am now married to a wonderful man that God has Blessed me with. I am also blessed with a wonderful daughter and 4 great grandkids